film posters of the 60s

the essential movies of the decade

from the reel poster gallery collection

edited by tony nourmand and graham marsh

 The Overlook Press
Woodstock • New York

First published in hardcover in 1998 by
The Overlook Press, Peter Mayer Publishers, Inc.
Lewis Hollow Road
Woodstock, New York 12498

Library of Congress Cataloging-in-Publication Data

Nourmand, Tony and Marsh, Graham.
Film posters of the 60s: the essential movies of the decade /
edited by Tony Nourmand and Graham Marsh.
p.   cm.
1. Film posters-Catalogs. I. Nourmand, Tony. II. Marsh, Graham.
PN1995.9.P5F46 1998 016.70143 75 09046-dc21 97-27374

Art direction and design by Graham Marsh
Page make-up by Trevor Gray

Manufactured in Singapore

Originally published in Great Britain by Aurum Press Limited

ISBN 0-87951-934-7

9 8 7 6 5 4 3 2 1

ACKNOWLEDGEMENTS

SPECIAL THANKS TO:
Richard Allen
Joe Burtis
Glyn Callingham
Tony Crawley
The Crew from the Island
Roxanna Hajiani
John Kisch
Bruce Marchant
June Marsh
Thomas Milne
Hamid Joseph Nourmand
Gabrielle Pantucci
Ken Schacter
Philip Shalam
Yasumasa Takahashi
X-Man

The Reel Poster Gallery
72 Westbourne Grove
London W2 5SH
Tel: +44 (0) 171 727 4488
Fax: +44 (0) 171 727 4499

Web Site: www.reelposter.com
Email: info@reelposter.com

contents

reelin' in the years

Invented by the Lumière brothers in 1885, the cinema has established trends and set people dreaming from the silent era to the present day. Although directors like Griffith, Eisenstein, Lang, Ford and Hitchcock were largely ignored by intellectuals of their day, their films are now at the heart of our culture. In fact, the cinema seems to have shaped the twentieth century more than any other art form.

Originally designed to attract attention and create desire, film posters were the principal way of telling people what was showing at their local cinema. Today, the imagery of the film poster has come to be known as 'key art'. It is expected to unlock, in perhaps sixty seconds or less, the heart of the film, while at the same time generating enough interest to open the public's wallet.

Posters would accompany the films they were designed to promote from one cinema to the next. Those that survived were returned to the distributors when the film's run had ended. With studios turning out an average of one film a week and always being cost-conscious, archiving this material was never a priority. In fact, when studio storerooms were full, film posters, having served their purpose, were usually destroyed. In other cases, extensive usage, wars, fires and all kinds of natural disasters have helped to make the vintage film poster scarce.

Today, as artefacts of an earlier period, movie posters are viewed in a different light. They are being collected by more and more people. For film buffs, they bring back nostalgic movie-going memories. The unique effect that comes from merging illustrations, lettering, layout and colour to create a 'movie-at-a-glance' image interests graphic designers. Historians and social scientists know that the study of films and their posters can provide significant insight into how our lifestyles and values have changed over time. The constant flux of fashions, prejudices, propaganda and social customs from distinctive and changing eras can all be found in film poster art. Encompassing, as it does, a vast range of styles and designs, the film poster appeals to an endless array of tastes.

Poster collecting is based on an almost naïve attraction to a combination of nostalgia, personal association, film and design appeal. In 1979, I purchased my first original film poster – an American poster

Dr. Strangelove Or: How I Learned To Stop Worrying And Love The Bomb (1964)
US 41 × 27 in. (104 × 69 cm)
Art by Tomi Ungerer

for *Apocalypse Now*. I was instantly hooked. I occasionally picked up duplicates and exchanged them with other collectors for material I really wanted. Over the past eighteen years, I have never stopped looking for posters. By 1992, my collecting habit had become a full-time job. My collector friend, Bruce Marchant, and I became completely absorbed by an exciting and adventurous paper chase. Our hunt took us around Europe and America and brought us face to face with horror stories of people casually overlooking film posters, most notably, a butcher in Oregon (also the owner of the local cinema) who was systematically working his way through posters from the turn of the century to wrap his meat. Needless to say, the one rare occasion where we do stumble upon a real gem makes the entire journey worthwhile and enables us to look back and laugh. With our pure delight in the film poster as an art form, we eventually conceived the idea of making them available to the gaze of those who have not yet experienced their enchantment. The Reel Poster Gallery, opened in 1995, was the result.

I met Graham Marsh last year through our mutual friend Glyn Callingham. I had seen and admired their book, *The Cover Art of Blue Note Records*. Graham expressed an interest in doing a series of books on film posters by the decade, focusing mainly on their design. The idea appealed to me since each volume would enable us to show posters of all film genres and types of design representing each individual decade. I believe that a 'good' poster not only portrays the film for which it was designed, but that ultimately its image perfectly represents the era in which it was born.

As was formerly the case with filmmakers, film posters and their designers never received the recognition which they deserved. Today, as well as being collectables, film posters are increasingly considered works of art and important historic documents.

Film posters of the 60s is the first in the series. By no means the ultimate selection, what follows is simply a small collection which we hope you will enjoy.

TONY NOURMAND

**Once Upon A Time In The West /
C'Era Una Volta Il West** (1969)
Italian 79 × 55 in. (201 × 140 cm)

C'ERA UNA VOLTA IL WEST CON **HENRY FONDA** **CLAUDIA CARDINALE** **JASON ROBARDS** NEL RUOLO DI ARMONICA **REGIA DI SERGIO LEONE** **GABRIELE FERZETTI** **CHARLES BRONSON** **PAOLO STOPPA** E IN ORDINE ALFABETICO TECHNICOLOR® TECHNISCOPE® **JACK ELAM** **LIONEL STANDER** **WOODY STRODE** **FRANK WOLFF** **KEENAN WYNN** UNA PRODUZIONE RAFRAN · S.MARCO

EURO INTERNATIONAL FILMS

hollywood hipsters, celluloid style …

In *Breakfast At Tiffany's* Audrey Hepburn's appearance as Holly Golightly brought a whole new meaning to pared down glamour. From the Givenchy-designed wardrobe of snappy little dresses to the huge lollipop shaped sunglasses, high-rise hair and kittenish attitude – a look just as desirable today as it was in 1961.

Movies have always had a habit of elevating everyday objects and clothes to cult status. On the big screen even the smallest details become as glamorous and cool as the stars that wear them.

Steve McQueen set the standard for cool as the anti-hero cop in *Bullitt*. Wearing a navy blue cashmere turtleneck sweater and driving a drab green 1967 390 GT fastback Mustang, he was the hippest police Lieutenant ever to hit the streets of San Francisco. It was a lethal combination. The out-of-town gunsels, in their black Dodge Charger, stood no chance when they went head to head with McQueen in the now-classic car chase. The streets of San Francisco were again safe until Lee Marvin, left for dead on Alcatraz, came back to demand his wedge of cash from the Organization in *Point Blank*. Their problem was Marvin did not accept credit cards … the town was once again steaming.

In 1962 Sean Connery as James Bond toppled two of America's biggest female icons, the young and beautiful Elizabeth Taylor and Doris Day, the eternal screen virgin. He became the biggest international star of the decade. Without a doubt Connery is entitled to the lion's share of credit for the success of James Bond. Turnbull and Asser, the famous men's clothiers on Jermyn Street, is where *Dr No* director Terence Young took Connery for his initial wardrobe. There

he was transformed by tailor Anthony Sinclair, from a Scots body-builder into the epitome of an English gentleman – albeit one with a licence to kill. Throw-away one-liners, assorted gadgets and drop-dead gorgeous women were standard issue in Bond films. But it was a silver Aston Martin DB-5 with modifications that was transported into the realms of mythology when driven by our cool hero in *Goldfinger*. In the early Bond films the combination of material and mechanical tailoring was impeccable, indeed invincible – nobody got the drop on 007.

At the other end of the spy movie spectrum, Michael Caine alias Harry Palmer grooved around London looking for *The Ipcress File*. With his unemotional dead-pan delivery, shorty raincoat and black framed glasses he must have been looking the other way as he passed James Bond's tailor. Not many people know this, but composer John Barry who wrote the Bond theme also scored the eerie music for *The Ipcress File*.

The 60s version of the 1930s according to Hollywood belonged to *Bonnie and Clyde*: they were fashion plates with a ba'ad attitude. No self-respecting fashion victim was safe from the duo's influence. The streets of every metropolis were filled to capacity with slinkily dressed, beret-wearing girls on the arms of men in pinstriped, wide-lapelled suits.

Barbarella did her thing in sexy space suits while Anthony Perkins' alter ego Norman Bates was taking care of business at the Bates Motel. In Hitchcock's *Psycho* he wore a corduroy Ivy League suit as sharp as his mother's knife. Meanwhile, across town Dustin

French 'New Wave' meets American Film Noir in **Le Samouraï**. (Detail from poster on page 73.)

Hoffman as *The Graduate* scored with Mrs Robinson sporting a seer-sucker jacket and button-down shirt – true Ivy Leaguers were rightly confused.

The decade surfaced some memorable romantic movies and one of the coolest was *Un Homme Et Une Femme (A Man And A Woman)*. Jean-Louis Trintigant and Anouk Aimee walking on the beach at Deauville in their stylish sheepskin coats and then climbing into, successively, Trintigant's red Mustang and a hotel bed – all to the accompaniment of a lush soundtrack by Francis Lai. The sales of teach yourself French books and sheepskin coats went through the roof.

The culture shock was seismic when *My Fair Lady* opened in the same year as The Beatles film *A Hard Day's Night*.... Musicals were in: none more elegant than *The Umbrellas of Cherbourg*. Ice queen Catherine Deneuve kept warm in a knee-length trenchcoat of which Thomas Burberry would have been proud. And he would certainly approved of Alain Delon's trenchcoat-wearing, existentialist hit-man Jef Costello, who had a passion for stealing Citroën DS's in Jean-Pierre Melville's classic masterpiece *Le Samouraï*.

Blow-Up, Antonioni's quintessential 'Swinging Sixties' movie had everything on the menu. Pop culture to go, complete with a side-order of great music from The Yardbirds a score by Herbie Hancock and clothes rails full of fab gear. Things happen to David Hemmings as a photographer caught in a passive life-style. He rubs shoulders with Vanessa Redgrave, snaps Verushka and cavorts with doe-eyed, white-lipsticked dolly birds. He even gets to watch a tennis match without a ball in sight. Like understatement.

Everyone smoked in 60s movies, from Eastwood's trademark cheroots to James Bond's Balkan and Turkish mixture cigarettes made for him by Morlands of Grosvenor Street. The black tobacco of Gitanes and Gauloises were the preferred smoke of the French 'New Wave' congregation while large cigars were de rigueur for the 'Mr. Bigs', high rollers and saloon keepers, and James Coburn without his Zippo lighter in *In Like Flint* would be like Miles Davis without his trumpet.

'What we've got here is a failure to communicate', a sentiment that did not apply sartorially to Paul Newman, who, as *Cool Hand Luke* was doing time in the hippest set of prison duds you've ever seen on a chain-gang. Unlike once upon a time in the west when even the humble poncho on the back of a squinting Clint Eastwood looked menacing. However some western movie experts are still convinced that director Sergio Leone supplied a bullet-proof poncho to Eastwood in *A Fistful of Dollars*.

Ironically, fashion from the 60s, in some form or other is back in vogue, and there is renewed interest in classic cars of the period. Even Minis, the true stars of *The Italian Job* have been updated for today's market, while original film posters that can still restore fading sixties memories to all those who tuned in, turned on, and dropped out are being elevated to cult status by a new generation of movie buffs. Like a wise old sage once said, 'What goes around, comes around'.

GRAHAM MARSH

**Les Parapluies De Cherbourg
(The Umbrellas Of Cherbourg)** (1964)
Japanese 60 × 20 in. (152 × 51 cm)

Cool Hand Luke (1967)
US 60 × 20 in. (152 × 51 cm)

The Graduate (1967)
US 41 × 27 in. (104 × 69 cm)
(Style B)

The Graduate (1967)
US 41 × 27 in. (104 × 69 cm)
(Style A)

JOSEPH E. LEVINE
PRESENTS
A
MIKE NICHOLS
LAWRENCE TURMAN
PRODUCTION

THE GRADUATE

STARRING
ANNE BANCROFT AND **DUSTIN HOFFMAN** · **KATHARINE ROSS**
SCREENPLAY BY
CALDER WILLINGHAM AND BUCK HENRY   SONGS BY PAUL SIMON
PERFORMED BY   PRODUCED BY
SIMON AND GARFUNKEL LAWRENCE TURMAN
DIRECTED BY
MIKE NICHOLS   PRINTS BY PATHE TECHNICOLOR® PANAVISION®
AN EMBASSY PICTURES RELEASE

The Cincinnati Kid (1965)
British 30 × 40 in. (76 × 102 cm)

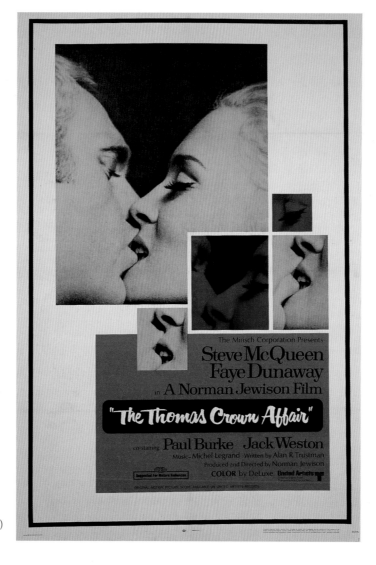

The Thomas Crown Affair (1968)
US 41 × 27 in. (104 × 69 cm)

Love With The Proper Stranger (1963)
US 41 × 27 in. (104 × 69 cm)

There is a moment—a long moment—
when everything is risked with the proper stranger.

NATALIE WOOD

STEVE McQUEEN

IN A **PAKULA-MULLIGAN** PRODUCTION

LOVE WITH THE PROPER STRANGER

WRITTEN BY ARNOLD SCHULMAN

Co-starring
EDIE ADAMS

Also
co-starring HERSCHEL BERNARDI and introducing TOM BOSLEY   Produced by ALAN J. PAKULA · Directed by ROBERT MULLIGAN · Music— ELMER BERNSTEIN · A PARAMOUNT RELEASE

L'Amour A 20 Ans (Love At 20)
(1962)
French 63 × 47 in. (160 × 119 cm)

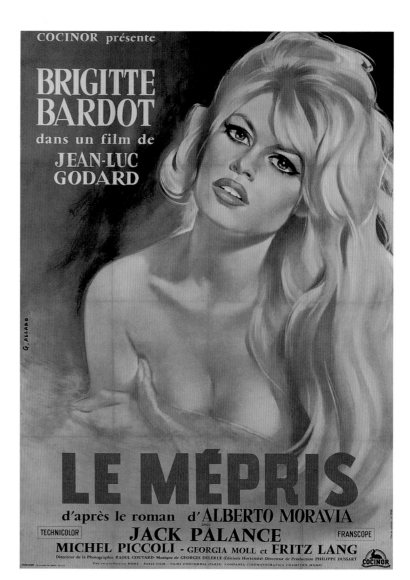

Le Mepris (1963)
French 63 × 47 in. (160 × 119 cm)
Art by Georges Allard

Belle De Jour (1967)
French 31 × 24 in. (79 × 61 cm)
Art by René Ferracci

Belle De Jour (1967)
Japanese 60 × 20 in. (152 × 51 cm)

**Breakfast At Tiffany's / Desayuno
Con Diamantes** (1961)
Spanish 39 × 28 in. (99 × 71 cm)
Art by Martí, Clave, Pico (MCP)

Un Homme Et Une Femme
(A Man And A Woman) (1966)
French 31 × 24 in. (79 × 61 cm)

Un Homme Et Une Femme
(A Man And A Woman) (1966)
US 41 × 27 in. (104 × 69 cm)

Un Homme Et Une Femme
(A Man And A Woman) (1966)
Japanese 30 × 20 in. (76 × 51 cm)

22

Cool Hand Luke (1967)
US 41 × 27 in. (104 × 69 cm)

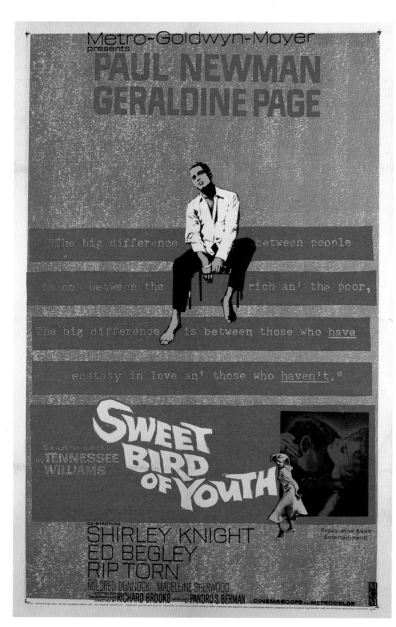

Sweet Bird Of Youth (1962)
US 41 × 27 in. (104 × 69 cm)

The Hustler (1961)
US 41 × 27 in. (104 × 69 cm)
(Re-release 1964)

The man...and the motion picture that simply do not conform.

PAUL NEWMAN

COOL HAND LUKE

CO-STARRING
GEORGE KENNEDY · J. D. CANNON · ROBERT DRIVAS · LOU ANTONIO · JO VAN FLEET
STROTHER MARTIN and
DIRECTED BY Stuart Rosenberg · PRODUCED BY GORDON CARROLL
SCREENPLAY BY DONN PEARCE and FRANK R. PIERSON · Music by Lalo Schifrin · TECHNICOLOR® PANAVISION® FROM WARNER BROS.-SEVEN ARTS

Copyright (c) 1967 Warner Bros.-Seven Arts Printed in U.S.A. 67/307

You never met a pair like Butch and The Kid

They're Taking Trains...
They're Taking Banks
And They're Taking
One Piece Of Baggage!

20th Century-Fox presents

PAUL NEWMAN
ROBERT REDFORD
KATHARINE ROSS

BUTCH CASSIDY A

A George Roy Hill—Paul Monash Production. Co-Sta
Executive Producer PAUL MONASH Produced by JOHN FORE
Music Composed and Conducted by BURT BACHARACH A NEWI

Butch Cassidy And The Sundance Kid
(1969)
British 30 × 40 in. (76 × 102 cm)

D THE SUNDANCE KID. 'A'

TROTHER MARTIN, JEFF COREY, HENRY JONES.

Directed by GEORGE ROY HILL Written by WILLIAM GOLDMAN

FOREMAN Presentation PANAVISION® COLOUR BY DE LUXE

Printed in England by Lonsdale & Bartholomew (Nottingham) Ltd.

Per Qualche Dollaro In Piu
(For A Few Dollars More) (1966)
Italian 37 × 26 in. (94 × 66 cm)
(Set of 3)

Per Qualche Dollaro In Piu
(For A Few Dollars More) (1966)
Italian 79 × 55 in. (201 × 140 cm)
Art by Franco Fiorenzi

Coogan's Bluff (1968)
US 22 × 14 in. (56 × 36 cm)

Midnight Cowboy (1969)
US 41 × 27 in. (104 × 69 cm)
Photograph by Steve Schapiro

Fistful Of Dollars (1964)
US 41 × 27 in. (104 × 69 cm)
(Advance)

The Wild Bunch (1969)
US 41 × 27 in. (104 × 69 cm)

A JEROME HELLMAN-JOHN SCHLESINGER PRODUCTION

DUSTIN HOFFMAN
JON VOIGHT

"MIDNIGHT COWBOY"

BRENDA VACCARO   JOHN McGIVER   RUTH WHITE   SYLVIA MILES   BARNARD HUGHES

Screenplay by WALDO SALT Based on the novel by JAMES LEO HERLIHY Produced by JEROME HELLMAN Directed by JOHN SCHLESINGER·
Music Supervision by JOHN BARRY "EVERYBODY'S TALKIN'" sung by NILSSON ORIGINAL MOTION PICTURE SCORE AVAILABLE ON UNITED ARTISTS RECORDS

COLOR by DeLuxe

 **X** PERSONS UNDER 17 NOT ADMITTED

 50 GO United Artists

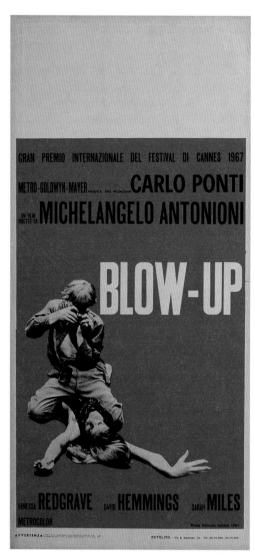
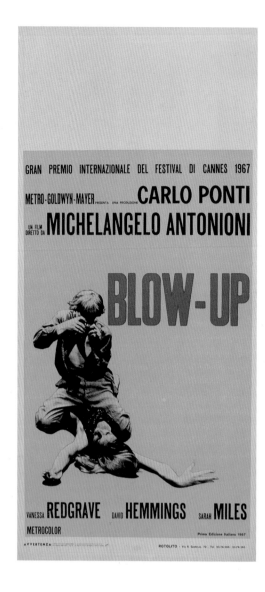
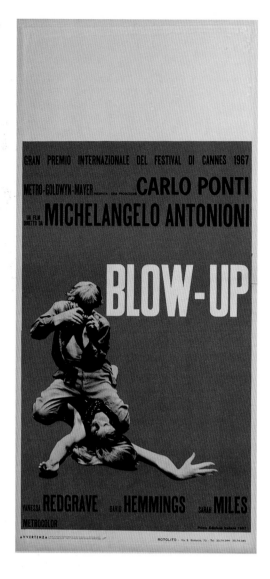

Blow Up (1967)
Italian 28 × 13 in. (71 × 33 cm)
(Set of 3)

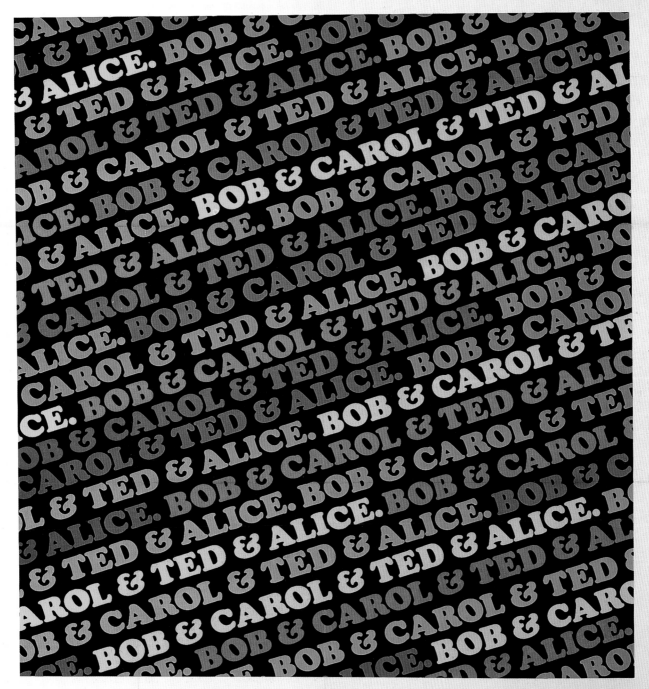

consider the possibilities

COLUMBIA PICTURES presents
A FRANKOVICH PRODUCTION

NATALIE WOOD   ROBERT CULP

BOB & CAROL & TED & ALICE

ELLIOTT GOULD   DYAN CANNON

Written by PAUL MAZURSKY and LARRY TUCKER • Music by QUINCY JONES
Executive Producer M. J. FRANKOVICH • Technicolor®
Produced by LARRY TUCKER • Directed by PAUL MAZURSKY

Soundtrack Album Available on Bell Records

Faces (1968)
US 22 × 28 in. (56 × 71 cm)

Chafed Elbows And Scorpio Rising
(1965)
US 41 × 27 in. (104 × 69 cm)
Art by David Weissmann

The Queen (1968)
British 30 × 20 in. (76 × 51 cm)

Film polski

nóż w wodzie

Reżyseria: Roman Polański

Produkcja: ZRF „Kamera"

Zdjęcia: Jerzy Lipman

W rolach głównych: Jolanta Umecka Leon Niemczyk Zygmunt Malanowicz

The Trip (1967)
US 41 × 27 in. (104 × 69 cm)

Acid - Delirio Dei Sensi (1968)
Italian 39 × 80 in. (99 × 203 cm)

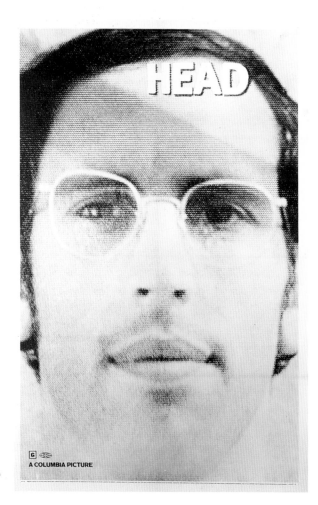

Head (1968)
US 41 × 27 in. (104 × 69 cm)
(Style C)

Prison (1965)
US 28 × 22 in. (71 × 56 cm)
(Mixed Media On Paper)
Art by Andy Warhol

Chelsea Girls (1966)
British 30 × 20 in. (76 × 51 cm)
Art by Alan Aldridge

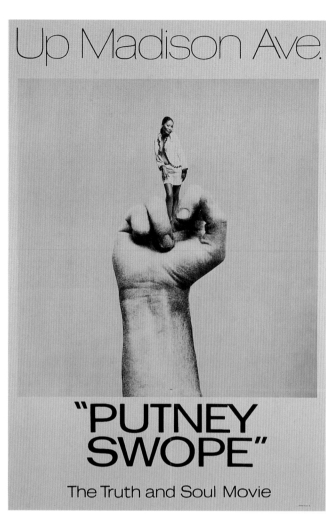

Putney Swope (1969)
US 41 × 27 in. (104 × 69 cm)

Mondo Cane / Pieski Swiat (1961)
Polish 33 × 23 in. (84 × 58 cm)
Art by Wojciech Zamecznik

The Cool World (1966)
US 41 × 27 in. (104 × 69 cm)

The Connection (1961)
British 30 × 40 in. (76 × 102 cm)
Art by Peter Strausfeld

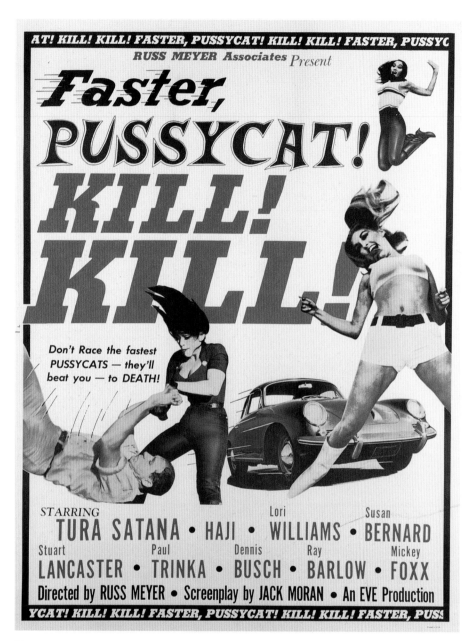

Faster, Pussycat! Kill! Kill! (1966)
US 41 × 27 in. (104 × 69 cm)

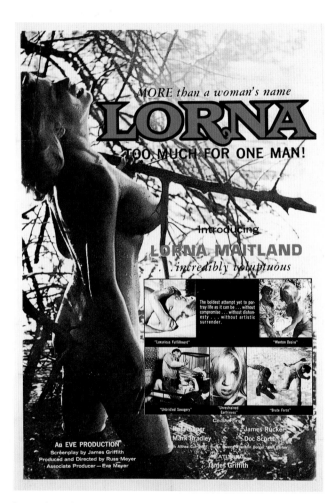

Lorna (1964)
British 41 × 27 in. (104 × 69 cm)

Girl On A Motorcycle (1968)
British 30 × 40 in. (76 × 102 cm)
(Style B)

'...a hand-grenade of a film... makes you laugh even as your blood chills... superb.'

EVENING NEWS

if....

Paramount Pictures Presents
A MEMORIAL ENTERPRISES FILM   Directed by LINDSAY ANDERSON   Screenplay by DAVID SHERW
ARTHUR LOWE   PETER JEFFREY   MONA WASHBOURNE   GEOFFREY CHATER   ANTHONY NICHOLLS introducing MALCO

ced by MICHAEL MEDWIN & LINDSAY ANDERSON Colour

WELL RICHARD WARWICK CHRISTINE NOONAN DAVID WOOD ROBERT SWANN

PRINTED IN ENGLAND BY W. E. BERRY LTD., BRADFORD

If.... (1969)
British 30 × 40 in. (76 × 102 cm)

46

Accattone (1961)
British 30 × 40 in. (76 × 102 cm)

La Notte (1960)
Italian 13 × 38 in. (33 × 97 cm)

L' Eclisse (The Eclipse) (1962)
Italian 28 × 13 in. (71 × 33 cm)

8½ (1963)
Italian 79 × 55 in. (201 × 140 cm)

Jules Et Jim (1961)
French 63 × 47 in. (160 × 119 cm)
Art by Christian Broutin

Vivre Sa Vie (1962)
French 23 × 15 in. (58 × 38 cm)
Art by Vaissier

Pierrot Le Fou (1965)
French 63 × 47 in. (160 × 119 cm)
Art by René Ferracci

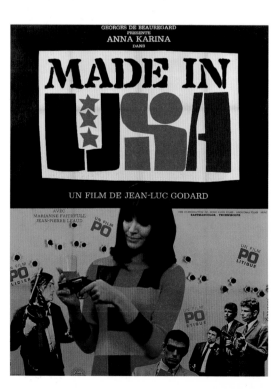

Made In USA (1966)
French 63 × 47 in. (160 × 119 cm)
Art by René Ferracci

PIERRE BRAUNBERGER

présente

ANNA KARINA

SADY REBBOT

HOTEL
INTERDIT AUX MOINS DE 18 ANS

VIVRE SA VIE

un film de
JEAN-LUC
GODARD

**PRIX SPÉCIAL DU JURY
ET PRIX DE LA CRITIQUE
AU FESTIVAL DE VENISE**

FILMS DE LA PLEIADE
95 Champs-Elysées-ELY.31-64

ATELIERS LALANDE   102, Rue Gabriel Péri, GENTILLY - ALE 16-71

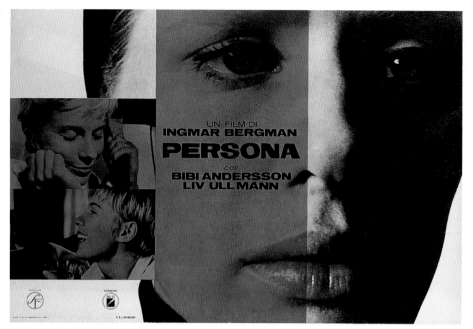

The Misfits (1961)
US 60 × 40 in. (152 × 102 cm)
(Special)
Photographs by Henri Cartier-Bresson,
Ernest Haas, Bruce Davidson, Cornell
Capa, Erich Hartman, Elliott Erwitt,
Dennis Stock, Eve Arnold, Inge Morath

Persona (1967)
Italian 19 × 27 in. (48 × 69 cm)
(Set of 3)

THE WORLD'S GREATEST PHOTOGRAPHERS SHOOT "the Misfits"!

Nine photographers from the international picture agency Magnum Photos, were assigned to cover the making of this important motion picture. Here each has chosen a photograph which captures the special excitement or mood of The Misfits and its stars.

Henri Cartier-Bresson
Ernest Haas
Bruce Davidson
Cornell Capa
Erich Hartman
Elliott Erwitt
Dennis Stock
Eve Arnold
Inge Morath

CLARK Gable MARILYN Monroe MONTGOMERY Clift in The John Huston Production the Misfits

CO-STARRING Thelma Ritter Eli Wallach SCREENPLAY BY Arthur Miller PRODUCED BY Frank E. Taylor DIRECTED BY John Huston MUSIC BY Alex North RELEASED THRU United Artists A Seven Arts Productions Presentation

This Sporting Life (1963)
British 41 × 27 in. (104 × 69 cm)
Art by Renato Fratini

Saturday Night And Sunday Morning
(1960)
British 30 × 40 in. (76 × 102 cm)

The Loneliness Of The Long
Distance Runner (1962)
British 30 × 40 in. (76 × 102 cm)
Art by S. John Woods

THE RANK ORGANISATION PRESENTS
A JULIAN WINTLE-LESLIE PARKYN PRODUCTION

RICHARD HARRIS
RACHEL ROBERTS

THIS SPORTING LIFE

Alan BADEL
William HARTNELL

SCREENPLAY BY DAVID STOREY

PRODUCED BY KAREL REISZ

DIRECTED BY LINDSAY ANDERSON

Printed in England.

The Servant (1963)
British 30 × 40 in. (76 × 102 cm)

A Taste Of Honey (1961)
British 30 × 40 in. (76 × 102 cm)
Art by E. Apicella

The Servant (1963)
Japanese 30 × 20 in. (76 × 51 cm)

Poor Cow (1967)
German 33 × 23 in. (84 × 58 cm)
Art by Fritz Fischer

Lolita (1962)
British 30 × 40 in. (76 × 102 cm)

Darling (1965)
British 30 × 40 in. (76 × 102 cm)

JEAN-PAUL BELMONDO • JEAN-CLAUDE BRIALY e ANNA KARINA

LA DONNA È DONNA

FRANSCOPE
EASTMANCOLOR

Regia: JEAN-LUC GODARD

Soggetto, adattamento e dialoghi di JEAN-LUC GODARD • Coproduzione italo-francese EURO INTERNATIONAL FILMS (Roma) - ROME PARIS FILMS (Parigi) • Realizzato da CARLO PONTI e GEORGES DE BEAUREGARD

13 Jours En France /
13 Dni W Grenoble (1968)
Polish 33 × 23 in. (84 × 58 cm)

Downhill Racer (1969)
US 41 × 27 in. (104 × 69 cm)
Design by Steve Frankfurt

The Endless Summer (1966)
US 17 × 11 in. (43 × 28 cm)

The Endless Summer

On any day of the year it's summer somewhere in the world. Bruce Brown's latest color film highlights the adventures of two young American surfers, Robert August and Mike Hynson who follow this everlasting summer around the world. Their unique expedition takes them to Senegal, Ghana, Nigeria, South Africa, Australia, New Zealand, Tahiti, Hawaii and California. Share their experiences as they search the world for that perfect wave which may be forming just over the next Horizon. **BRUCE BROWN FILMS**

Bruce Brown Films the producer of "Slippery When Wet," "Surf Crazy," "Barefoot Adventure," "Surfing Hollow Days," "Waterlogged" and "The Endless Summer."

Le Testament D'Orphee (1960)
French 63 × 47 in. (160 × 119 cm)
Art by Jean Cocteau

Repulsion (1965)
British 30 × 40 in. (76 × 102 cm)
Art by Jan Lenica

Cul De Sac (1966)
British 30 × 40 in. (76 × 102 cm)
Art by Jan Lenica

Camelot (1967)
US 41 × 27 in. (104 × 69 cm)
Art by Bob Peak

The Fox (1968)
US 41 × 27 in. (104 × 69 cm)
Art by L. & D. Dillon

The Illustrated Man (1969)
British 30 × 40 in. (76 × 102 cm)

Rosemary's Baby (1968)
US 41 × 27 in. (104 × 69 cm)
Design by Steve Frankfurt

**La Maschera Del Demonio
(Black Sunday)** (1960)
Italian 79 × 55 in. (201 × 140 cm)
Art by Giuliano Nistri

Whatever Happened To Baby Jane?
(1962)
US 41 × 27 in. (104 × 69 cm)

Kill Baby Kill (1969)
US 41 × 27 in. (104 × 69 cm)

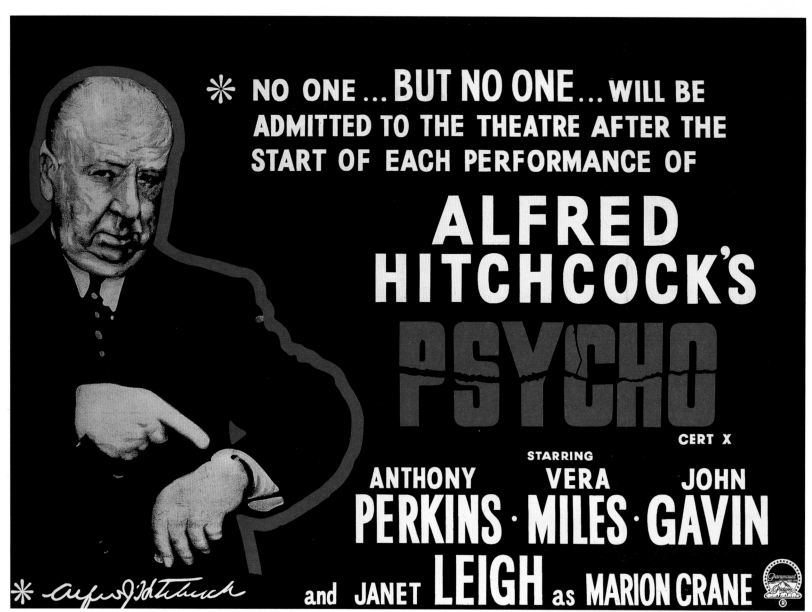

Psycho (1960)
British 30 × 40 in. (76 × 102 cm)
(Style B)

Psycho / Psyco (1960)
Italian 55 × 39 in. (140 × 99 cm)

Peeping Tom (1960)
British 30 × 40 in. (76 × 102 cm)

68

Dracula Prince Of Darkness (1965)
British 30 × 40 in. (76 × 102 cm)

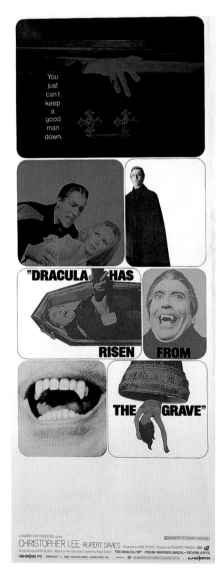

Night Of The Living Dead (1968)
British 30 × 40 in. (76 × 102 cm)

Dracula Has Risen From The Grave
(1968)
US 36 × 14 in. (91 × 36 cm)

THEY WON'T STAY DEAD!

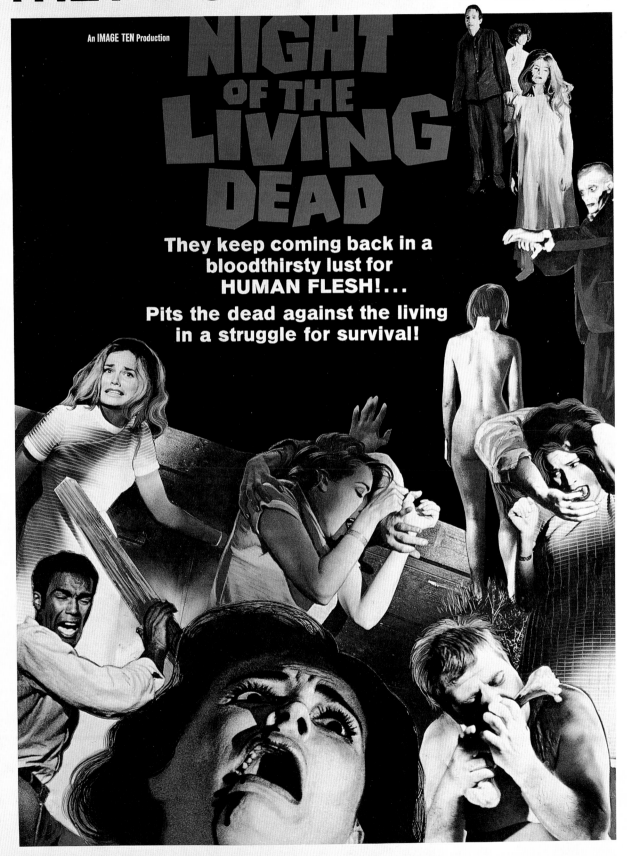

An **IMAGE TEN** Production

NIGHT OF THE LIVING DEAD

They keep coming back in a bloodthirsty lust for **HUMAN FLESH!**...

Pits the dead against the living in a struggle for survival!

Starring **JUDITH O'DEA · DUANE JONES · MARILYN EASTMAN · KARL HARDMAN · JUDITH RIDLEY · KEITH WAYNE**

Produced by Russel W. Streiner and Karl Hardman · Directed by George A. Romero · Screenplay by John A. Russo · A Walter Reade Organization Presentation — Released by Continental

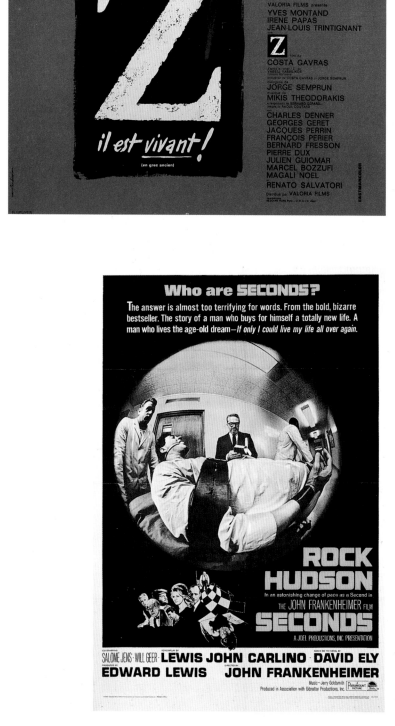

Z (1969)
French 31 × 24 in. (79 × 61 cm)

Alphaville (1965)
French 63 × 47 in. (160 × 119 cm)
Art by Jean Mascii

The Manchurian Candidate (1962)
US 41 × 27 in. (104 × 69 cm)

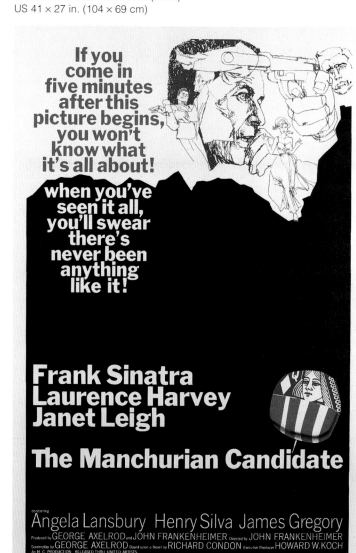

Seconds (1966)
US 41 × 27 in. (104 × 69 cm)

Le Doulos (1962)
French 31 × 24 in. (79 × 61 cm)
Art by Jacques Fourastie

Le Samouraï (1967)
French 63 × 47 in. (160 × 119 cm)
Art by René Ferracci

LE SAMOURAÏ

PRODIS présente

| ALAIN DELON |

un film de
JEAN-PIERRE MELVILLE

LE SAMOURAÏ

avec

FRANÇOIS PERIER
et
NATHALIE DELON

production
FILMEL - FILMS BORDERIE - T.C.P.
FIDA CINÉMATOGRAFICA

Producteur délégué : EUGÈNE LEPICIER

Photo de : HENRI DECAE

Bullitt (1968)
US 41 × 27 in. (104 × 69 cm)
(Advance)

Bullitt (1968)
Italian 79 × 55 in. (201 × 140 cm)
Art by Ferrini

Bullitt (1968)
US 41 × 27 in. (104 × 69 cm)
(Style A)

BULLITT comes to this theatre soon. That ought to shake up the place pretty good.

Not many freaky cops like BULLITT around. You look at the Italian shoes and the turtleneck and you have to wonder. You listen to the official beefs about 'personal misconduct,' 'disruptive influence,' you figure he's got to be up for trade.

But when some rare Chicago blood starts spilling in San Francisco, they give BULLITT the mop. They weren't exactly doing him a favor. But they've done a great big one for you.

STEVE McQUEEN AS 'BULLITT'

ROBERT VAUGHN

JACQUELINE BISSET · DON GORDON · ROBERT DUVALL · SIMON OAKLAND · NORMAN FELL

M SUGGESTED FOR MATURE AUDIENCES

Music by Lalo Schifrin · Screenplay by ALAN R. TRUSTMAN and HARRY KLEINER · Based on the novel "Mute Witness" by Robert L. Pike · Executive Producer ROBERT E. RELYEA · Produced by PHILIP D'ANTONI · Directed by PETER YATES · TECHNICOLOR® FROM WARNER BROS.-SEVEN ARTS W

69/11

Robbery (1967)
British 30 × 40 in. (76 × 102 cm)

Oceans 11 (1960)
US 36 × 14 in. (91 × 36 cm)

You
wouldn't
call it a gang.
Just Danny Ocean
and his 11 pals –
the night they blew
all the lights in Las Vegas!...

TECHNICOLOR® PANAVISION PRESENTED BY WARNER BROS.

78

Bonnie And Clyde (1967)
US 41 × 27 in. (104 × 69 cm)

The Rise And Fall Of 'Legs' Diamond
(1960)
British 30 × 40 in. (76 × 102 cm)

WARREN BEATTY
FAYE DUNAWAY

They're young... they're in love

...and they kill people.

BONNIE and CLYDE

MICHAEL J. POLLARD · GENE HACKMAN · ESTELLE PARSONS

Written by DAVID NEWMAN and ROBERT BENTON · Music by Charles Strouse · Produced by WARREN BEATTY · Directed by ARTHUR PENN

TECHNICOLOR® FROM WARNER BROS.-SEVEN ARTS

The Ipcress File (1964)
British 30 × 40 in. (76 × 102 cm)
(Style A)
Design by Eric Pullford

Point Blank / Zbieg Z Alcatraz (1967)
Polish 33 × 23 in. (84 × 58 cm)
Art by Bronislaw Zelek

Metro-Goldwyn-Mayer presents
A Judd Bernard-Irwin Winkler
Production starring
LEE MARVIN
"POINT BLANK"

There are two kinds of people in his up-tight world:
his victims and his women. And sometimes you can't tell them apart.

co-starring **ANGIE DICKINSON**
KEENAN WYNN · CARROLL O'CONNOR · LLOYD BOCHNER · MICHAEL STRONG
Screenplay by Alexander Jacobs and David Newhouse & Rafe Newhouse   Based on the Novel "The Hunter" by Richard Stark
Directed by John Boorman · Produced by Judd Bernard and Robert Chartoff   **In Panavision® and Metrocolor**

Alfie (1966)
British 30 × 40 in. (76 × 102 cm)

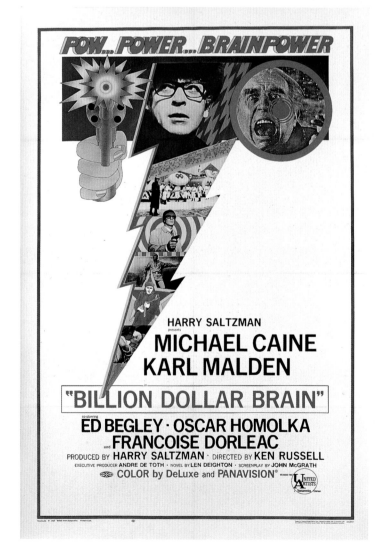

Billion Dollar Brain (1967)
US 41 × 27 in. (104 × 69 cm)

Birdman Of Alcatraz (1962)
US 36 × 14 in. (91 × 36 cm)
Art by Saul Bass

"THEY GOT A MURDER ON THEIR HANDS.
THEY DON'T KNOW WHAT TO DO WITH IT."

THE MIRISCH CORPORATION Presents

SIDNEY POITIER   ROD STEIGER

in THE NORMAN JEWISON · WALTER MIRISCH PRODUCTION

"IN THE HEAT OF THE NIGHT"

co-starring
WARREN OATES
LEE GRANT

Screenplay by
STIRLING SILLIPHANT

Produced by
WALTER MIRISCH

Directed by
NORMAN JEWISON

COLOR by DeLuxe   MUSIC – QUINCY JONES · "IN THE HEAT OF THE NIGHT" sung by RAY CHARLES

Suggested For Mature Audiences   ORIGINAL MOTION PICTURE SOUNDTRACK AVAILABLE ON UNITED ARTISTS RECORDS

UNITED ARTISTS
Transamerica Company

Batman (1966)
British 30 × 40 in. (76 × 102 cm)

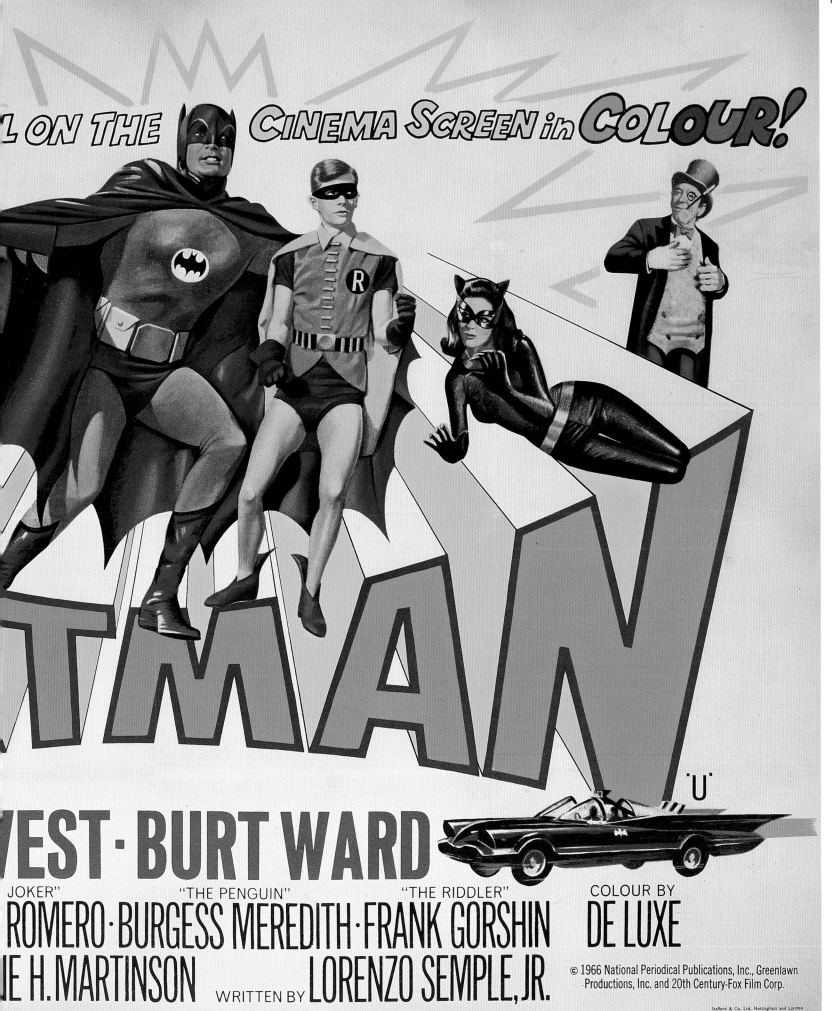

2001: **A Space Odyssey** (Cinerama)
(1968)
US 41 × 27 in. (104 × 69 cm)
(Style C)
Art by Robert McCall

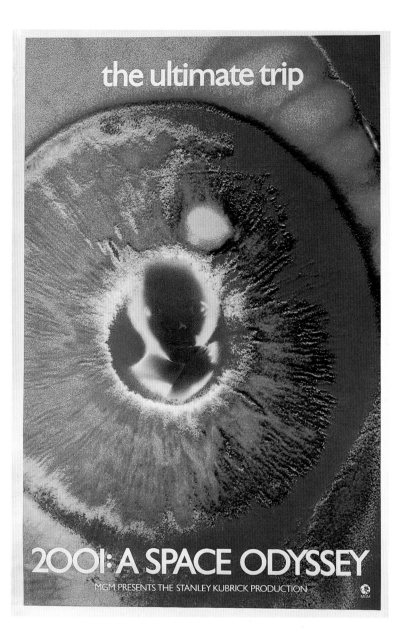

2001: **A Space Odyssey** (1968/69)
US 41 × 27 in. (104 × 69 cm)
(Style D)

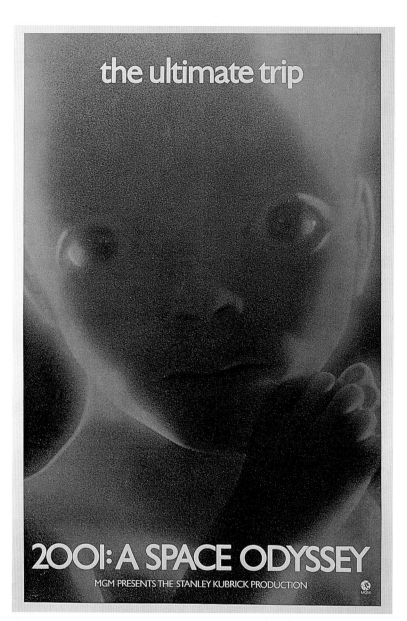

2001: **A Space Odyssey** (1968/69)
US 41 × 27 in. (104 × 69 cm)
(Style E)

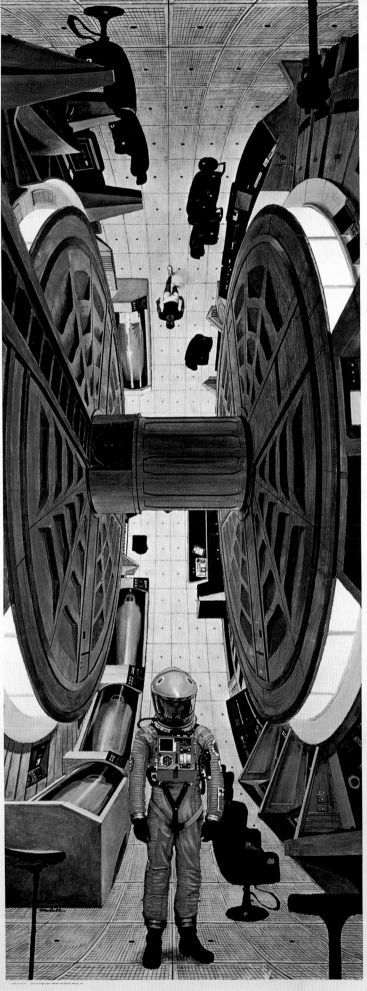

An epic drama of adventure and exploration

...taking you half a billion miles from Earth... further from home than any man in history. Destination: Jupiter.

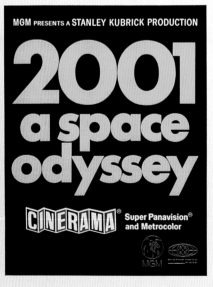

MGM PRESENTS A STANLEY KUBRICK PRODUCTION

2001 a space odyssey

CINERAMA® Super Panavision® and Metrocolor

Fantastic Voyage (1966)
US 41 × 27 in. (104 × 69 cm)

Fantastic Voyage (1966)
US 22 × 14 in. (56 × 36 cm)
(Special Advance)

Terrore Nello Spazio
(Planet Of The Vampires) (1965)
Italian 28 × 13 in. (71 × 33 cm)
Art by Averardo Ciriello

The Time Machine (1960)
British 30 × 40 in. (76 × 102 cm)

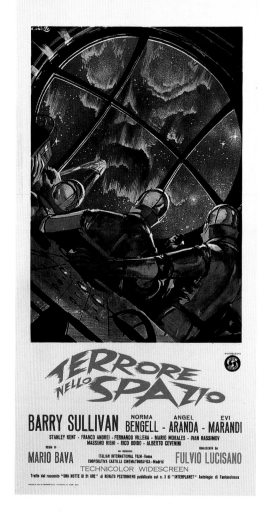

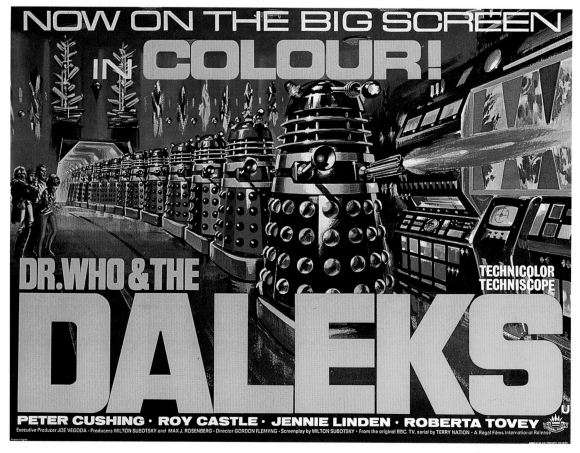

Dr. Who And The Daleks (1965)
British 30 × 40 in. (76 × 102 cm)

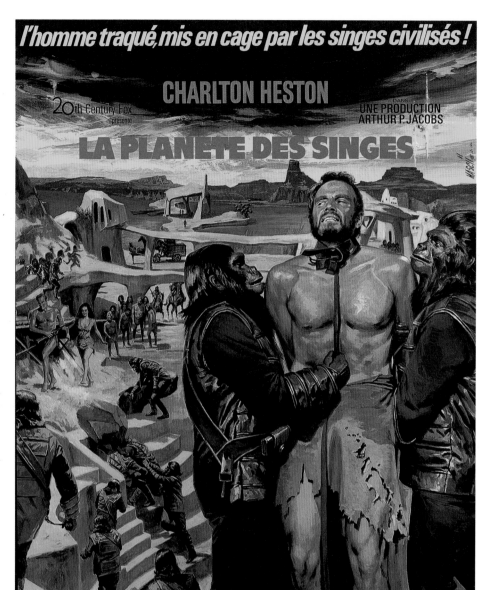

**Planet Of The Apes /
La Planete Des Singes** (1968)
French 31 × 24 in. (79 × 61 cm)
Art by Jean Mascii

Planet Of the Apes (1968)
British 30 × 40 in. (76 × 102 cm)

CHARLTON HESTON
w amerykańskim
filmie przygodowym
Reżyseria:
Franklin J. Schaffner
w pozostałych rolach:
Roddy Mc Dovall
Kim Hunter
Maurice Evans

PLANETA MAŁP

96

The Longest Day (1962)
US 81 × 41 in. (206 × 104 cm)

Hell In the Pacific (1969)
British 30 × 40 in. (76 × 102 cm)

42 INTERNATIONAL STARS!

DARRYL F. ZANUCK'S

**THE
LONGEST
DAY**

FROM THE BOOK BY
CORNELIUS RYAN
RELEASED BY
20.
Century-Fox

The Great Escape (1963)
British 30 × 40 in. (76 × 102 cm)

Where Eagles Dare (1968)
US 36 × 14 in. (91 × 36 cm)

TRAIN THEM! EXCITE THEM! ARM THEM!

...THEN TURN THEM LOOSE ON THE NAZIS!

In 70 mm. wide screen and full stereophonic sound!

METRO-GOLDWYN-MAYER presents A KENNETH HYMAN PRODUCTION

The Dirty Dozen

Starring **LEE MARVIN** **ERNEST BORGNINE** **CHARLES BRONSON** **JIM BROWN** **JOHN CASSAVETES** **RICHARD JAECKEL**

GEORGE KENNEDY **TRINI LOPEZ** **RALPH MEEKER** **ROBERT RYAN** **TELLY SAVALAS** **CLINT WALKER** **ROBERT WEBBER**

screenplay by **NUNNALLY JOHNSON** and **LUKAS HELLER** From the novel by **E.M. NATHANSON** Produced by **KENNETH HYMAN** Directed by **ROBERT ALDRICH** IN **METROCOLOR**

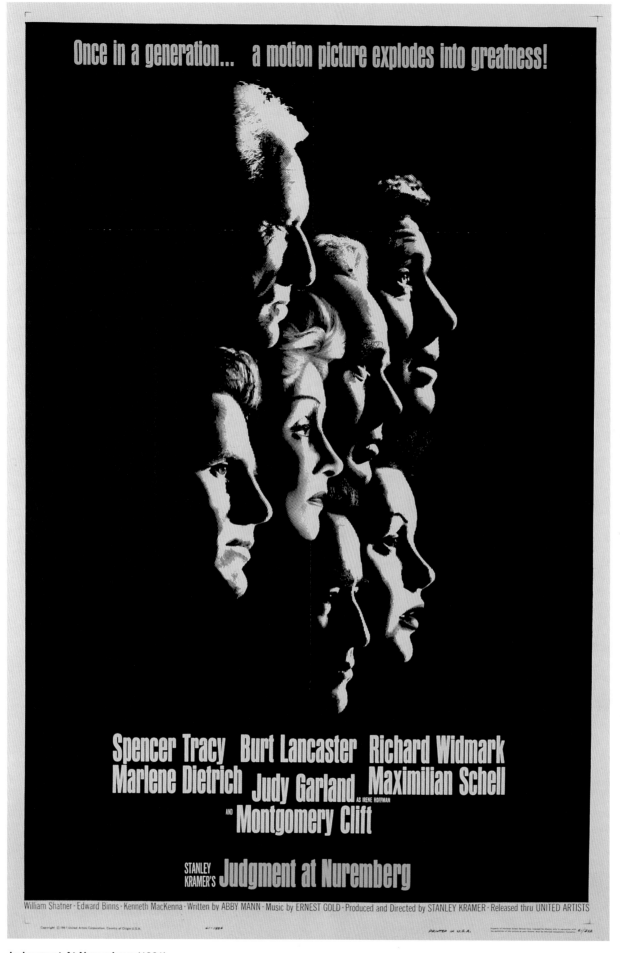

Judgement At Nuremberg (1961)
US 41 × 27 in. (104 × 69 cm)

Lawrence Of Arabia (1962)
US 41 × 27 in. (104 × 69 cm)
(Roadshow)

From the creators of "The Bridge On The River Kwai."
Columbia Pictures presents The SAM SPIEGEL · DAVID LEAN Production of

LAWRENCE OF ARABIA

"I deem him one of the greatest beings alive in our time.
...we shall never see his like again. His name will live in history.
It will live in the annals of war...It will live in the legends of Arabia!"
—WINSTON CHURCHILL

STARRING
ALEC GUINNESS · ANTHONY QUINN
JACK HAWKINS · JOSE FERRER
ANTHONY QUAYLE · CLAUDE RAINS · ARTHUR KENNEDY
AND INTRODUCING
PETER O'TOOLE as 'LAWRENCE' WITH OMAR SHARIF as 'Ali'
SCREENPLAY BY ROBERT BOLT · PRODUCED BY SAM SPIEGEL · DIRECTED BY DAVID LEAN · TECHNICOLOR® A HORIZON PICTURE IN

PHOTOGRAPHED IN
SUPER PANAVISION 70®

Red Beard / Rudobrody (1965)
Polish 33 × 23 in. (84 × 58 cm)
Art by Stanislaw Zamecznik

Cleopatra / Kleopatra (1963)
Polish 33 × 23 in. (84 × 58 cm)
Art by Eryk Lipinski

Japoński dramat psychologiczny AKIRY KUROSAWY

RUDOBRODY
Nagroda za kreację TOSHIRO MIFUNE na Festiwalu w Wenecji

Produkcja: Toho

104

The Miracle Worker (1962)
US 41 × 27 in. (104 × 69 cm)

Lilith (1964)
US 22 × 28 in. (56 × 71 cm)

'the Miracle Worker'

DESIGN: TRINKAUS, ARON & WAYMAN

a great motion picture starring Anne Bancroft and introducing Patty Duke

Victor Jory with Inga Swenson, Andrew Prine & Kathleen Comegys. Screenplay by William Gibson based upon his stage play.
Music composed by Laurence Rosenthal. Produced by Fred Coe. Directed by Arthur Penn. Released thru United Artists

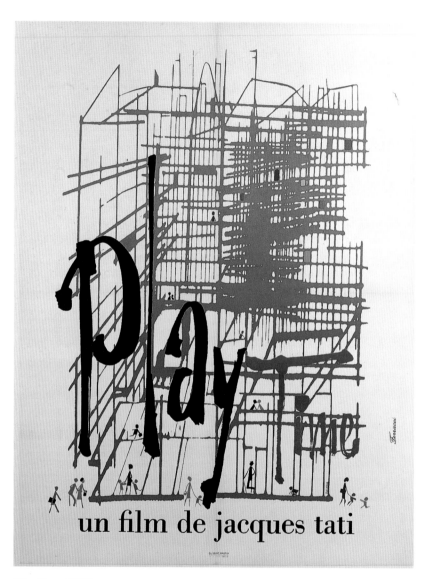

French Dressing (1963)
British 41 × 27 in. (104 × 69 cm)

Play Time (1967)
French 31 × 24 in. (79 × 61 cm)
Art by Baudin
Design by René Ferracci

'68年ベネチア映画祭O.C.I.C賞／女優演技賞■シルバーナ・マンガーノ／テレンス・スタンプ主演■監督ピエル・パオロ・パゾリーニ　カラー作品

音楽エンニオ・モリコーネ／主題曲〈サントラ盤〉キング・レコード／撮影ジュゼッペ・ルッツォリーニ／イタリア映画■東和提供

猥褻の美学か──
官能の芸術か──
鬼才パゾリーニが
世界に叩きつける
はげしい衝撃！

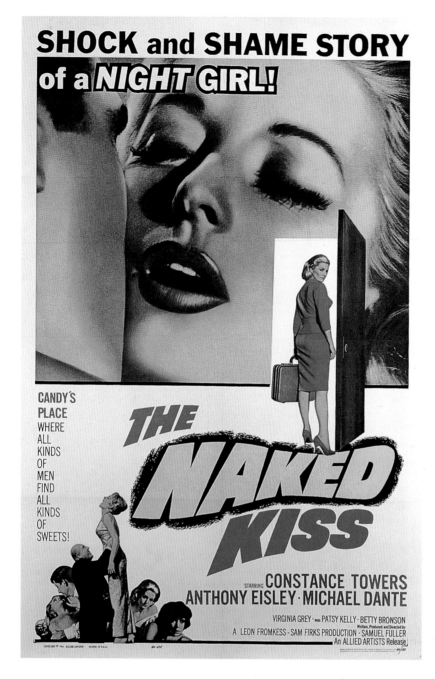

The Naked Kiss (1964)
US 41 × 27 in. (104 × 69 cm)

Irma La Douce (1963)
British 30 × 40 in. (76 × 102 cm)

Goldfinger (1964)
British 30 × 40 in. (76 × 102 cm)
(Style A)

110

JAMES BOND BACK IN ACTION !

ALBERT R. BROCCOLI & HARRY SALTZMAN PRESENT

SEAN CONNERY AS JAMES BOND 007

IN IAN FLEMING'S

GOLDFINGER Ⓐ

HONOR BLACKMAN AS PUSSY GALORE
GERT FROBE AS GOLDFINGER

TECHNICOLOR®

UNITED ARTISTS

SCREEN PLAY BY RICHARD MAIBAUM & PAUL DEHN

PRODUCED BY HARRY SALTZMAN & ALBERT R. BROCCOLI

DIRECTED BY GUY HAMILTON   EON PRODUCTIONS LTD

Dr. No (1962)
British 30 × 40 in. (76 × 102 cm)

Thunderball (1965)
British 30 × 40 in. (76 × 102 cm)

From Russia With Love (1963)
British 30 × 40 in. (76 × 102 cm)
Art by Renato Fratini

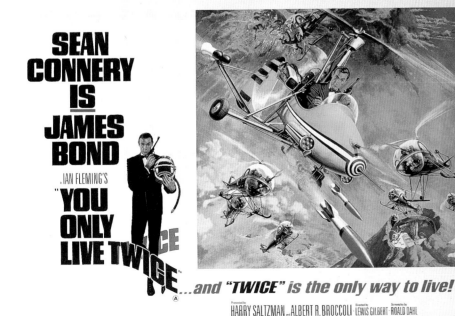

You Only Live Twice (1967)
British 30 × 40 in. (76 × 102 cm)
(Style B)

Casino Royale (1967)
US 60 × 20 in. (152 × 51 cm)
(Set of 6)

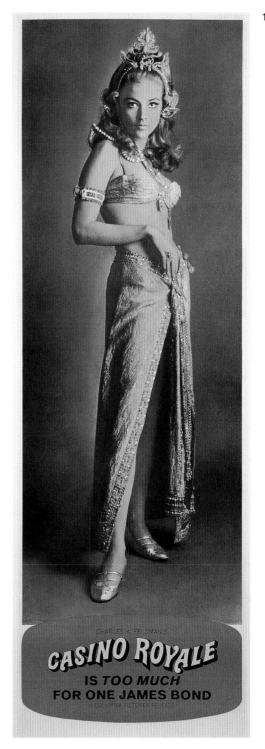

Casino Royale (1967)
US 22 × 14 in. (56 × 36 cm)

116

The President's Analyst (1967)
US 41 × 27 in. (104 × 69 cm)

Modesty Blaise (1966)
US 41 × 27 in. (104 × 69 cm)
Art by Bob Peak

In Like Flint (1967)
US 41 × 27 in. (104 × 69 cm)
Art by Bob Peak

Un Chien Andalou (1928)
French 47 × 32 in. (119 × 81 cm)
(First Release 1968)
Art by Francisco Fernandez Zarza
(Jano)

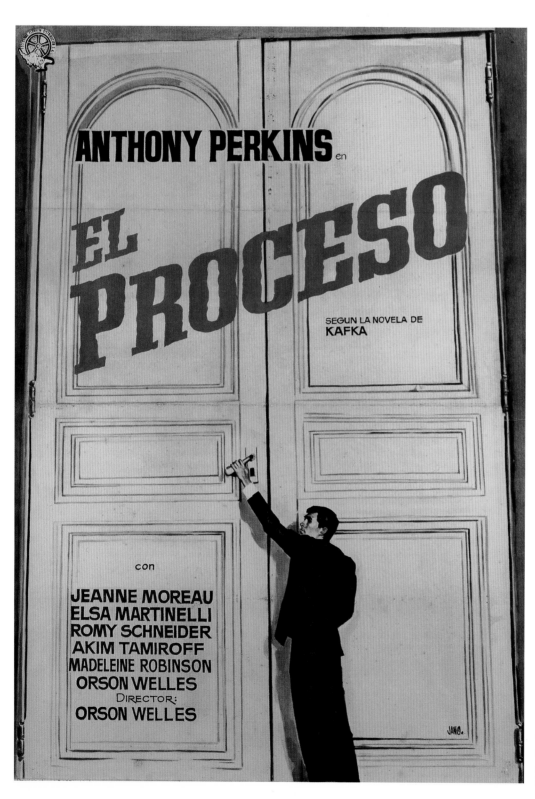

The Trial / El Proceso (1962)
Spanish 39 × 28 in. (99 × 71 cm)
Art by Francisco Fernandez Zarza
(Jano)

UN CHIEN ANDALOU

UN FILM DE LUIS BUÑUEL ET SALVADOR DALI

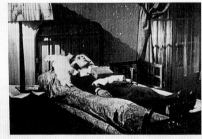

120

My Fair Lady (1964)
Italian 27 × 36 in. (69 × 91 cm)
(Style A)
Design by Ferrini
Photograph by Cecil Beaton

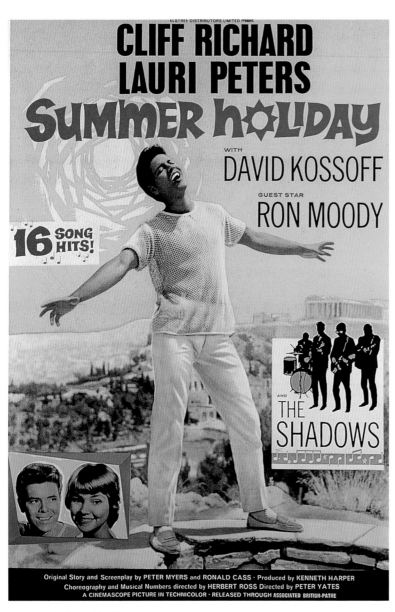

Summer Holiday (1962)
British 41 × 27 in. (104 × 69 cm)

Get Yourself A College Girl (1964)
US 41 × 27 in. (104 × 69 cm)

THE SCREEN ACHIEVES ONE OF THE GREAT ENTERTAINMENTS

IN THE HISTORY OF MOTION PICTURES

MIRISCH PICTURES PRESENTS

"WEST SIDE STORY"

A ROBERT WISE
PRODUCTION

STARRING NATALIE WOOD

RICHARD BEYMER   RUSS TAMBLYN
RITA MORENO   GEORGE CHAKIRIS

DIRECTED BY ROBERT WISE AND JEROME ROBBINS SCREENPLAY BY ERNEST LEHMAN
ASSOCIATE PRODUCER SAUL CHAPLIN / CHOREOGRAPHY BY JEROME ROBBINS
MUSIC BY LEONARD BERNSTEIN LYRICS BY STEPHEN SONDHEIM
BASED UPON THE STAGE PLAY PRODUCED BY ROBERT E. GRIFFITH AND HAROLD S. PRINCE
BOOK BY ARTHUR LAURENTS
PLAY CONCEIVED, DIRECTED AND CHOREOGRAPHED BY JEROME ROBBINS
PRODUCTION DESIGNED BY BORIS LEVEN / FILMED IN PANAVISION® 70 / TECHNICOLOR®
PRESENTED BY MIRISCH PICTURES, INC. / IN ASSOCIATION WITH SEVEN ARTS PRODUCTIONS, INC.
RELEASED THRU UNITED ARTISTS

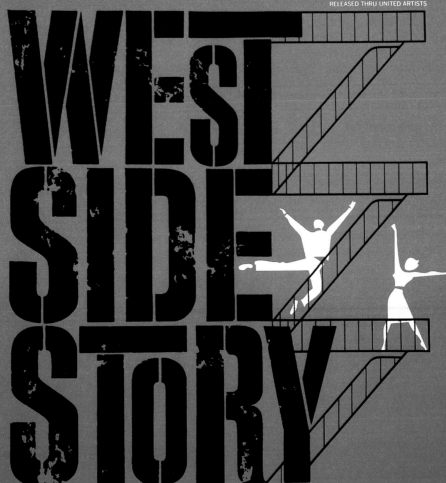

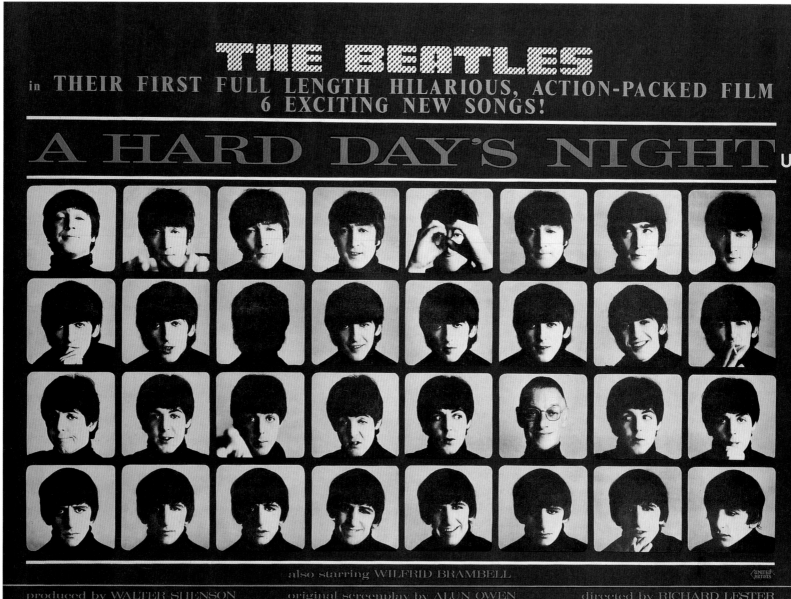

A Hard Day's Night (1964)
British 30 × 40 in. (76 × 102 cm)
Design & Photography by Robert
Freeman

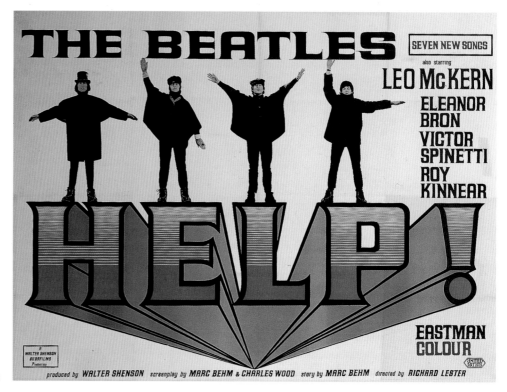

Help! (1965)
British 30 × 40 in. (76 × 102 cm)

Yellow Submarine (1968)
British 30 × 40 in. (76 × 102 cm)
Art by Heinz Edelmann

Easy Rider (1969)
US 41 × 27 in. (104 × 69 cm)

Monterey Pop (1969)
US 41 × 27 in. (104 × 69 cm)
Art by Tomi Ungerer

Easy Rider (1969)
Italian 19 × 27 in. (48 × 69 cm)

Don't Look Back (1967)
US 41 × 27 in. (104 × 69 cm)

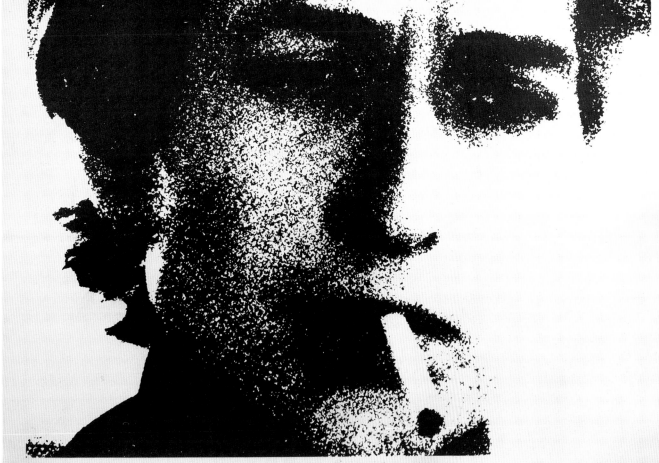